OCEAN

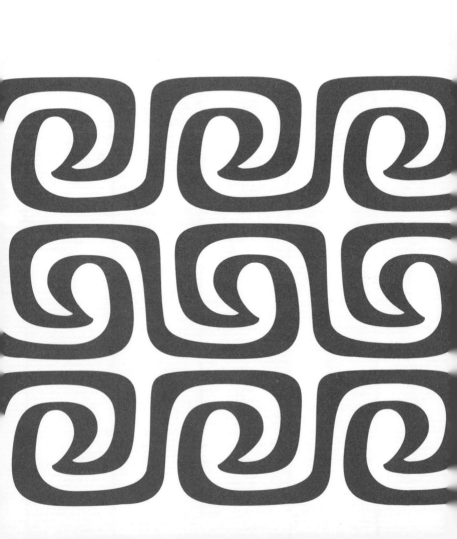

OCEAN

Poems by Sue Goyette

GASPEREAU PRESS ¶ PRINTERS & PUBLISHERS ¶ MMXIII

I don't want to be the oldest performer in captivity ...
I don't want to look like a little old man dancing out there.
FRED ASTAIRE

We traded an accordion of hours for wood. We traded ladles
of sleep for some hammers and nails. We were setting out

to find the ocean. Our boats leaked. Our boats sank.
Our boats needed to be trained. We burned some of them

for light to build better boats. We turned some on their sides
and lived in them. Our children wrote their names in crooked

letters on the backs of them. Someone even cut a hole in the centre
of one and wore it suspended like pants. For awhile, everyone

wore boats. We built more fashionable boats. We wrote books
about building boats and then wrote more about the writing

of those books. Sure, we digressed but there was always plenty
of wood and a prime-time of hours to trade. A colony of us left

to watch how light moved over our boats. This demanded clocks.
We banged on our boats and howled and in this way created

the Calling of the Ocean ceremony. This became a holiday
with a feast and a fire. Dancing. Our population almost doubled

when we drank the fermented fruit and holidayed. We cleared more
land to store the boats. The boatbuilding industry was booming.

We eventually even cooked our boats and ate their ash
then dreamt at night of fish. Fish. Those strange contraptions

that don't need air. Little wallets swimming just out of reach.

We soon had an orchestra of boats and the songs
that sailed through us put the stars in the sky.

Of course, we were nowhere near the ocean. Our trees
were nuns at the edge of our plans, praying for us

in their way. And our rocks were mysteries we tried solving
but in these parts, the rocks are as stubborn as sisters and held

their tongues. We corded off part of a field beyond our beds
where the right combination of drink and wind

would leave us feeling oceanated. This land later became
a church then later, a music hall. Sacred. There were expeditions

to find the ocean. The reports given upon return always involved
leaping animals and thirst. There was first a swamp of skyscrapers

to cross, a swarm of bankers. There were small shields
called briefcases and banks where you had to wait to be given

what belonged to you in the first place. At this point,
the bigger boats became stages and these journeys would be acted out

for everyone to see. Often children would be cast as bankers
shielding themselves with those briefcases. They'd run around at a silent

movie speed, begging everyone for more money. I played a skyscraper
but my arms got tired so I was replaced. Once I played a tree.

You're not praying hard enough, the audience heckled.

The real estate agent chewed gum to cover the smell
of bank on his breath and told us a snow fence would keep it

out. That it wasn't so much like student housing
but a wishing well that would one day increase

our property value. Oceanfront was like 24-hour shopping;
we'd browse its surface and wonder who really needed

all this stuff. And what a hurricane of a question!
What a tidal wave of disruption. It got worse

when we walked into it and let it taste us. Courtship!
We had never heard of marriage let alone ceremony.

When we wrote our names in the soft sand of its back,
we didn't know the first thing about commitment

or about being out of our depths.

It won every staring contest. Would laugh
at our jokes. It was the original god of hypnosis

and made us all feel sleepy. Over time, it became
a breed of static, an out-of-service channel broadcasting

beyond our buildings. If we drove to its feet,
it wasn't to confront it, but more to adjust

our own reflections, straighten out our hearts with the old
if-you-know-what's-good-for-you talk. Sure, our grandmothers

insisted on throwing in gifts of false teeth and single shoes
but reverence was considered a form of weakness

and we decided the ocean was a daring but
equally fashionable accessory for our vacation wardrobe.

The art of complaint was perfected when we first took note
of its temperature.

THREE

Halifax, once the capital of the medieval fog trade,
still has its ancient fog-making bellows. These bellows

look like cannons which explains the unfortunate
misunderstanding all those centuries ago between

the fog workers and the Haligonian shadow sculptors.
The dispute lasted for years and, often at dusk,

there'd be a showdown that resulted in barroom brawls
and heartbreak. One dark November, there was a shortage

of shadows and only gasps of fog left. Street venders
sold cheap imitations, throwing cups of tea at people's feet

and declaring the wet street their new shadow.
Unfortunately, these shadows were steadfast which defied

the real purpose of nomadic darkness. Replicas of fog
were easier to spot. Men often glued cotton on sticks

or stood, arms outstretched, billowing out white sheets.
When they moved, they'd move slowly as if rolling in

from the ocean. This did create jobs but also elicited catcalls
and debauchery from their women. Real shadows were made

across the harbour back then, in Dartmouth. The refinery
still stands and ancestors of lurking shadows gone feral

can still be seen in its parking lot and across the street
in Value Village. Value Village isn't a real village

but a metropolis of used clothing where fog stitched into
the hems and sleeves of old raincoats can still be found.

This is the unspoken history of our city. Fog was responsible
for many marriages and, consequently, when it lifted,

many in-laws.

We first invented running so we could be in two places
at one time but then understood how, with empty pockets,

we could also harvest the wind. We invented hospitality
to lure our successes home, and to get love a much-needed

drink. We invented chairs so we could rest after the chase.
We invented the chase after we invented running, and inadvertently,

robbery. We invented the suburbs after accidentally colliding
into the feud and its conniving stepsisters the argument

and the snit. Some of us needed more space.
We discovered death under the bridge

and someone insisted we take it home, that it needed
our help. That day alone we invented the handkerchief

and the whisper. When it sat up, when it looked at us
with the teeth of its appetite puddinged in its eyes, we discovered

the flapping of words trying to escape from our ears
and something hammering in the silver-shaft of our hearts.

We unearthed fear that day, our first act of real
archeology. Understand, at that point, maps charted roads

and the humble footpaths between rumours crooked
with love. The ocean took up the most room

with its tidal pull and tentacled beasts inventing
their own recipes. Some days we knew we were nothing

but ingredients; other days we felt like honoured guests.
But the day we brushed the dirt from fear's forehead

and got a look at its hands, well, our maps changed
and the ocean got bigger, our nights, a great deal beastier.

The incline to our streets was first invented
as an easy way to feed the ocean tethered

to the end of them. We'd roll down bottles
of the caught breath of our gifted sermons.

We'd drag skeins of dream talk. Little hoofed
arguments. The ocean was a beast left in our care

and it was in our best interest to keep it fed.
This is how we thought back then. For awhile

it was renamed Dragon and men would spear its sides
and endure its wrath to get to the swimming jewels

beneath it. We often ate those jewels,
cooking their slender bodies over our fires.

Back then, we didn't know a great deal
about dragons and how, when provoked,

they'd stand and flap their gigantic wings.
This is how we first learned of storms. The fish

in our cooking pots would swim hard then,
the lash of their home coming down for them

through our roofs.

It acted like it had something
to say. We'd find trunks of broken

wine glasses, crab claws poised to attack
whatever had pulled them apart. We were truly

bewildered. Some of us were dreaming
of the same old crone who begged us to bend

and untangle her memories. Some of us worked
at jobs that involved filing complaints

about noise in the same cabinet as proposed
ideas for a better city. We had only just begun

to put leashes on things that had resisted
being caught. In this way, we muzzled

our concerns and decided to turn on lights
before it got dark. We spent many hours

learning to sing with the open throats
of lilies. But we were restless. The crone

in our dreams cackled at our impatience
and started a fire in the kitchens of our childhoods.

We'd wake up smelling smoke and longing to be held
by our bedtimes again. We ate copious amounts

of shadows cast by heritage buildings. There was a safety
in numbers but no one wanted to head in the same

direction. We were alone, the way the ocean was alone
and briefly we understood why it couldn't find the right words

for what it wanted to say and why it kept trying.

We had laughed at first. At the thought. Like it was
a joke. Imagine, the ocean *basting* us. But how often

had we walked into its salted air then licked our arms
to taste it later? We were being seasoned. Lightly. Of course we rebelled,

refusing to be in its roasting pan. But we had never encountered anything
so stubborn. It was worse than a mountain, its altitude

ranging in the upper echelon of *I know you are but what am I?*
And it was stoic, like a four-year-old la, la, la-ing. I can't hear you, it said.

The artists claimed it was the quintessential canvas.
Call it love, they insisted, and look how love persists. The widows said:

call it death or call it loneliness. Whatever it was, it was vast and swam
in its lane at the edge of our town without ever resting. It shouldn't have

come as such a surprise then, at how tender we were all becoming
and how close we were cooked to tears.

The trick to building houses was making sure
they didn't taste good. The ocean's culinary taste

was growing more sophisticated and occasionally
its appetite was unwieldy. It ate boats and children,

the occasional shoe. Pants. A diamond ring.
Hammers. It ate promises and rants. It snatched up

names like peanuts. We had a squadron of cooks
specifically catering to its needs. They stirred vats

of sandals and sunglasses. They peppered their soups
with pebbles and house keys. Quarts of bottled song

were used to sweeten the brew. Discussions between
preschool children and the poets were added

for nutritional value. These cooks took turns pulling
the cart to the mouth of the harbour. It would take four

of them to shoulder the vat over, tipping the peeled
promises, the baked dreams into its mouth.

And then the ocean would be calm. It would sleep. Our mistake
was thinking we were making it happy.

The idea of home was so big, so bottomless,
carpenters had to tie a rope around their waists

for fear of being swallowed whole by the houses
they were building. They burned sawdust

mixed with invoices addressed to their mothers'
maiden names and inhaled the smoke

of homesickness until it seeped into their dreams.
The first hinge was a replication of a scarab beetle,

half of its insect legs holding onto the idea of coming,
the other half holding onto the idea of going.

Hammers were the original instruments
for the nomadic walking song and installing windows

was a master class on marriage counselling. A good
carpenter was worth her weight in forest.

A rudimentary way of testing a carpenter's skill
was to get her to walk amongst trees. A carpenter

with a heavy hand, an inability to appreciate
the future footsteps on the floorboards she was laying

would literally make the trees shirk.

It was like our shyness had escaped its rabbit cage.
We were talking to everyone! The streetlights,

those scholars, had very little to say about transcendence
but would show us by coming on right when we were

mid-sentence. There was an immigration of questions
plowing our thoughts and harvesting our sleep.

We had come to realize we understood next to nothing!
The poets, it turned out, were our compasses but their pace

was slow; the longer their metaphors steeped in the dark,
the more potent they'd be when they finally did use them

and we could vouch for that. Many of us were still
intoxicated by a poem we'd heard. We only had to say

the word *wolf* again and our pre-ancestral fur would singe,
the paws of our joy bounding off the path and, gratefully,

we would find our yodel. Thankfully our songwriters wrote songs
that managed to put us to sleep though they did us no favour

by bringing up the ocean again after we'd been trying
so hard to quit it.

We weren't introduced to bees until someone
overheard them and mistook their drone

for a school board meeting. Naturally she didn't
bother getting any closer because those days

the talk at school board meetings may have sounded
grand but it all boiled down to using less art

to paint more arithmetic. The bees, we'd discover later,
were miniature flying lions. Sure, their growl

was small but they were onto something. Our engineers
sketched the kind of motors we'd need to achieve

the same flight patterns and quickly kiboshed
the idea when they realized they needed cosmic dust

from somewhere like the ring of Saturn to achieve
the bees' dizziness. It was the long talks they'd have

with our flowers we were most curious about.
The way they rubbed their paws as if the plan

they were hatching with the marigolds was delicious.
Or diabolical. Later, when we tasted their honey,

we realized they weren't miniature flying lions at all
but small winged gospels sent to sweeten our tongues

and instigate a new flowering kindness in our talk.
In this way, they were hugely responsible for compliments

and the beginning of our population boom.

TWELVE

One of the first ceremonies women invented was to yell louder
for someone to bring them more rain. They banged

at the drought as if it were a door that the whole world
was hiding behind. Then they tried softening their voices

with frosting from the gratitude they'd feel if someone,
anyone, brought them more rain. They chiselled their shrieks

with the thistles of their thirst and the dry land of their tongues.
Listen, they commanded to the empty room, *we really need*

more rain. Sometimes they forgot and one of them would sing
of the caravan of sadness and what she'd left behind.

Their sorrow would harmonize then and they'd become a choir
for injustices. In this way, they won the support of the earth

and the deep rumble of its voice put stones and canyons
in their songs. The trees, those paradoxes of escape

and capture, had a similar thirst and voted to consolidate
with the choir and in doing so, allowed the women to see

the blueprints of green for the first time. The women
realized then that their demands were in fact holy.

They said the word prayer for the way it zippered open
the silence. They said the word thirst for the way the heart tires

of sanding down the day to see the ingrain of truth.
It wasn't until the early morning, when men woke to empty beds

and children to empty bowls, that the idea of women
and their choir was entertained let alone taken seriously.

THIRTEEN

The idea of courting began after a group of us
smoked the exhaust from a pride of children

imagining they were lions. We wouldn't normally
smoke something that potent but the night had begun

to pontificate, droning on like a politician
promising us more day. Some of us were feeling

a little hemmed in. Understand, the strongest
we were used to smoking was the echo

of a good laugh so this feeling of having paws
and a home as far as our growls could reach

was something new. At first our prowl
was self-conscious. The way we'd nudge

into each other. We blushed at the sharp teeth
of being touched. Of course, everything changed

when we discovered our purr.

FOURTEEN

Our women were the first to need intervention.
They'd been spending their late afternoons

drinking rainwater and now had wet stones
in their talk. Everything looks better wet,

they'd pronounce to the chagrin of their husbands
but to the delight of the bachelors. It was the ocean

that insisted they get out of their clothes. It was the ocean
that taught them to turn up the sand in their whispers.

Pandemonium was at high tide in those days
and women were insisting on diving into every wave.

In this way, we learned about the undertow
of flirting, the grit of heartbreak and how it can get into

places you didn't even know you had.

We grew alarmingly quiet the years we believed
our heartbreak had made the ocean salty. We had found

love like a box of candles beneath our beds
and lit each other with the flame of our tongues.

We had no idea how love would go on to build its fires
in our every word. How it's a factory that churns out action

in a way that our slow-moving city wasn't used to.
Oh, the high school musical of a smile. The conquest

and lasso of a kiss. We learned to play the fiddle
in those days because, honestly, we really needed something

to do with our hands. Just the thought of each other
made our beds too big and our chimneys chug more smoke.

The city turned on its streetlights so we could find each other
in the dark. Love is like that. It knocks on doors

and urges you to vote. It stands on the corner
and croons a cover tune of promises. We found ourselves

giving it everything we had, so when it left, we didn't just cry
of its leaving but for how much of ourselves it took with it.

We realized then that we lived on a peninsula and the rocking
for water surrounding us was actually the ocean

slurping.

There were many stories about what was going on
beneath its surface. Some prayed to the perpetually

weeping girl who sat in a rocking chair on the creaking
of its floor and nursed her sadness like offspring.

When the ocean's surface was still, they believed
she'd stopped rocking and was waiting by a lobster trap

for her sister to come home. It was her loneliness
that fished the waters for our swimmers, for our sailors.

All their voices crammed in her cellar are what we sometimes
heard. It's why we drank, the way they knew our names,

the demands they made, insidious as the wind coming through
our windows, fussing with our hair.

Those who didn't get enough to eat were convinced
beneath its surface was a banquet. It was the motherland

of mothers bending over our sleeping deaths and tucking in
the cold feet of our adventurers. When pressed,

we named her *Mer*: the unlocked door of her heart ajar
for our shyness, a sunken treasure of welcome-homes

mapped to be found. Her hands knotted the hours into days
and lit candles for the orphans that had made camp in the stairwells

of their hope. The way she spread her hush over the storm
of our worries, the way she smoothed the rocks of our hard days.

If it was an ache that she wouldn't let us stay,
it was an ache that preened itself soft like glass.

Beneath the ocean is a pacing old man
who can no longer look at himself in the mirror.

He sits at his kitchen table with his back to his
shore. Ignoring his daughters who bring soup

to his bowl, who bring song to his silence.
His sons have all gone off and become finned.

They have forgotten the way he'd read to them,
the way he taught them of the breath. His wife

swallowed a hook and was abruptly married
to someone else. The sound of his heart breaking

inspired teacups and violins. When his brothers
were alive, they'd visit with empty suitcases

and smuggle away as much of his dark mood as they could.
It may be true, after those visits, if you were lucky

enough to be standing on shore, there was the glimmer
and then the glow of something swimming

or chasing its own tail. Either way, for a moment,
you drowned in something, for lack of a better word,

called joy.

SEVENTEEN

The ocean is the original mood ring.
Often, and for days, it convinced us

we felt an industrial grey malaise with a deep heart
of blue. The occasional whip of a whitecap idea

would bloom in our plans. We'd sit by its side
while it slept, our pens poised like fishing rods.

When it granted an interview, it refused to talk
about its film credits or its accolades of full moons.

It was more interested in talking about what we thought
it tasted like: fish or tears, it wanted to know.

And it loved stalking us. Some of us would wake
with that rear-view feeling of being watched. We'd skid out

of our dreams only to sink over our heads. When we could,
we'd spear a good conversation and carry it, wriggling,

to its mouth. We'd find the bones of what we were trying
to say later, washed up on shore. We'd boil them to drink

their broth then wake hungover from the truth. Some days,
the ocean would convince us we were green

with many small ambitions, and other days we were used
aluminum foil, an offshore of seagulls dipping

and stealing morsels of our memories. In this way, we knew
we were aging. Some days, if we were to believe it, we felt

nothing but a progress of sky, a fleet of spaceships shaped
like clouds sailing out of our harbour in search of somewhere new.

Some believed the ocean wasn't always salty but that our ancestors
had been very sad. They'd been promised a great many things

only to have the fruit drop and their breasts sag. They cried
a lot. When they looked up and bemoaned their fate,

claiming they'd done nothing to deserve all of this roadkill,
the exhaust from their undeservedness formed a talk show

of rain clouds. When they looked upon the ground
and beseeched their feral happiness to stop chewing

at their feet, their displeasure seeded gout weed and prehistoric
thorned things. In this way, our boats were the original forms

of escape and self-help. At first we floated on our ancestors' sadness,
the waters rife with the salt of their tears, but then,

vivre l'evolution, those tears sprouted gills and tails
and small, watchful eyes. It isn't entirely accurate to say

we ate those fish but more like accepted that which we'd inherited.
What we hadn't anticipated was how the eyes of those original tears

would persist, how they'd keep watching.

NINETEEN

The weather has always been both a concern
and conversation kindling. We took great pride

in how long we could talk about a single cloud.
To some it looked like a ringing phone,

to others it looked marsupial. Special teams
would inject needles into its shade, testing the samples

in their laboratories. Life, we voted, would be easier
if we knew what was going to happen. This was the biggest

flaw and became the complaint that motored
many meetings. Exactly who was in charge?

And why weren't they letting us prepare?
Fashion designers collapsed into meltdowns:

was the trench coat going to make a comeback
or would we be stuck forever with these pullover things?

The poets chose to dip their pens in the silence
of not knowing and wrote letters to the future

in small stanzas that often resolved themselves
with images of birds. Even our children, tall as they were,

couldn't see anything coming our way. And the ocean,
well, the ocean was a failed experiment. We could drop

a whole house into it in exchange for what it knew.
It was moving all right but still

it wouldn't budge.

Oh, little clouds over Halifax, if you must continually rain
on us, rain then your blessings. This is how most city meetings

would start. We'd discuss making new lanes
for the smooth-talkers because they'd often instigate parades.

We'd argue about the feral minute balanced between each day
and who gets to claim it. We'd debate the ownership of the wind

above a fence at a property line and who could harness it. We
were important and doing busy work. Often these meetings

would go on for many hours. Someone was selling cans
of fog and someone else was claiming the fog was fake.

Someone wondered which blade to use when carving
fog and how much funding the fog carvers should receive.

Understand, the city was bustling and though the harbour
was not yet bridged, our ideas were leaping across

its water. Dartmouth wasn't just our sister city then
but an opportunity for more holidays and a new political

platform. If we were night, Dartmouth was a top hat.
If we were an apple, it was the à la mode. Poets wrote

comparisons without compensation until an anthology
was published under the guise of a public transportation map

and then even the poets were quiet. It felt like there was nothing
left to say. Some of us bought black market canned fog

and stayed up late drinking it. The clouds over Halifax
could no longer be addressed as little. The ocean was a dominatrix.

We tied up our boats and created a 24-hour hotline for those of us
it handcuffed into sleep. We couldn't even trust our shadows,

that thing they did, always straining towards the water.

Each of us had a ferry making the tumultuous crossing
from our hearts to our mouths and vice versa. A sturdy vessel

of intent that had carved the shortest passage between silence
into the crowded rush hour of talking. It took great courage

to embark from a dense forest where love acted like a fox
or a badger scuttling along unnoticed and arriving somewhere

paved in language lit with skyscrapers of promise and a pollution
of fear. This ferry from our hearts to our mouths was responsible

for some of our greatest adventures. *Adieu, I do,* and that sort of thing.
Inspired, we invited a group of children and octogenarians

to design a vessel we could use to travel the equally necessary passage
between Halifax and Dartmouth. They didn't want to work

it turns out. We then asked a group of politicians and zookeepers
who quickly established a tax and feeding schedule then elected

a lemur to not only revise their budget but to let out the sound
they'd been secretly feeling when asked to do anything. The poets

described an aerial egg-shaped capsule guided by a spine of cable
to symbolize the rebirth we'd experience every time we arrived.

The choir chose the A minor key for departure and an uplifting
B major for arrival, a bit of a march with a hint of overture.

We weren't getting anywhere until we asked the happily married couples.
What surprised us was their practicality accessorized by passion.

Make it watertight, they insisted, but give it lots of windows
for the moon to get in.

TWENTY-TWO

Some politicians wanted a wider shore so more people
could visit our city. They had their architects draw up

plans that would tether the water back and stretch the sand
thinner. There were formulas that considered the length

of our recline with the necessary amount of grains of sand.
This was the grandfather of tourism. They also considered

large mirrors to reflect more sun and misting the air
with more salt to instigate a bigger thirst. The slabs

of rocks, however, were proving to be a better organized
protest than we could ever arrange. The bankers funded

good weather campaigns and a fleet of back hoes.
The rocks, dangling mid-air, were mammoth, the shock

of their underbellies, their ineffectual tusks. They were dropped
in a field outside of town that was quickly renamed

a geological museum complete with a rest area and entrance fee.
This may have taught us about progress, but the ocean

was teaching us about patience. It was compelling to see it
take its time, stretching its slow hunt, nursing new rocks.

TWENTY-THREE

The more it ate of us, the less we liked it.
It wasn't rocket science. It was loss.

Its reach astounded our fences, rushed
into our basements like a hold-up. It was its own

getaway car. Some days it was a diva.
Petulant. It demanded a spotlight. It gargled

before it sang. We made the mistake of treating it
like the original pet and leashed it with wharves.

Or we'd take pictures of it like it was a starlet getting out
of a limo. We followed the soap opera of its life,

the tumultuous affair it was having with the moon,
its battle with addictions. Its violence. It would leave us

broken, making excuses for its temper. It was part pirate,
part pantry. We figured out later it must have studied a trade,

a career it could fall back on. In seconds it could find
our fuse box and re-route our wiring. In this way, the ocean

was schooled on how to light us up and then power surge us
back into darkness.

TWENTY-FOUR

The original lifeguards were taught to address the ocean
as neighbour. *Neighbour,* they'd said, always showing

their open hands, *please give back the child you've
swallowed.* They were also counselled to end the day

with a lit candle held up then blown out in case the ocean
had not yet learned of rest. Lifeguards were considered

masters with an innate ability to mediate. Each time
they encountered a hostage situation, they encountered

a different family member of their own terror. Their voices
hardly had the time to transform to bird and hover

above the waves let alone fish for movement, that last clasp
of mouth with breath. The pressure of that moment

was responsible for a kind of spiritual collapse that would take
centuries to resuscitate. You could say we turned our back

to the ocean then. Purposefully built houses to face the sun
and then invented curtains to keep that out as well.

We grew inward and managed to fulfill the old prophesy
by addressing those of us who dared to swim rather than

the hungry ocean itself.

TWENTY-FIVE

Someone had figured out how to grind up footprints
and then sold them by the gram. It only took snorting

a few lines to wake up a homesickness we hadn't
experienced before. This elicited its own kind of hangover

that made our feet feel like tired tongues, the long story
they'd been telling mapped now and given street names.

We were guilty of putting up fences. We were guilty
of lawn care. We were guilty of pruning our lilac ideas

until they could no longer flower; of weeding the wilderness
from the turnips of silence that grew beneath us,

pale and verging on purple. Despite all of this,
our young children still insisted on riding us like horses,

holding our hair when we tried bucking them off.
You could say they were little vitamins for our imagination.

We transformed into ghosts for them,
haunting the hallways while they wiggled in bed,

caught between terror and a cayenne kind of glee.
We were rehearsing for something, we just didn't know what.

TWENTY-SIX

The barbers taught us how to trim the trees.
They'd say *careful of their ears,* proving something

we'd all suspected. A farmer came to show us how to use
the chainsaw. *Say your names,* he said above the banshee

of its teeth. *That's how long it takes.* This is now a steadfast
rule about a lot of things though at the time all we could imagine losing

was a limb. The trees knew we were coming. You could feel them
cower. Our best day was following the grade one class

learning of habitat. The trees were giddy, all those hands
on their knees, the tree jokes the children were practising:

Leaf me alone, leaf me alone! They practically bent down
for us. But some of us had to retire early. We knew how trees

could hear everything, the way they spiced the breeze,
even with the names we had kept hidden.

TWENTY-SEVEN

Resuscitating a tree takes great skill. The poets
had recorded the original ceremony but wrote it

with ink brewed from the spruce's potent shade,
and though the taste was still faint, we, unfortunately,

could no longer read it. Using the aspen rhyme scheme
as a clue, for a long while, we believed the first line

must end with *free*. Or *melody. Parapluie.*
We were a little desperate and consulted the lifeguards

who suggested swimming with the current then holding
each tree around its trunk and dragging it back to shore.

There is an admirable single-mindedness to mastery
that mustn't be belittled so we paid them handsomely

for their advice. We then consulted with our seniors
but they didn't see anything wrong with the trees

and insisted we just leave them alone so they all could watch
their shows. Our children had grown so tall, they no longer

could hear us. It was when one of our farmers laid his hands
on the back of a maple that we noticed the tree perk up.

You have to understand what it is to graze, he told us, *and what it is
to rest.* His hand was a plowed field and picked berries.

Sometimes it was a running stream and sometimes it was
a bucket. He kept it on the tree for the whole hour he told us

what he knew of land and by the time he left, we could tell
if the maple had been able to, it would've just up and left with him.

TWENTY-EIGHT

We recruited sturdy lawn chairs and consulted
an architect before placing them on the shore.

Our aim was simple, we wanted to welcome
what the ocean had to tell us and make amends

with it. We wanted the chairs to display our willingness
but also our resolve. We would not be pushed around.

We could only find eight lawn chairs that stood the test
of tide. We advertised it as a master class of listening.

One woman, in response, baked a cake. A carpenter
mailed us a pinecone. We couldn't help but press

the fourth grader's poem about spring to our lips,
tasting the daffodil of its optimism. A miner

sent a flashlight. A mathematician sent a violin.
And a security guard sent his father's cough,

dried like fruit leather. A widow sent her late husband's laugh
distilled into five drops, one for each decade they'd been married.

And an insomniac sent a pillow stuffed with the grass
from the field she no longer dreamt about. Our chairs were filled.

For a long time, the ocean slept. Our fourth grader
insisted he could hear its dreams of swimming trucks

delivering the colour blue and shark fins. There were lights
in its stomach and sometimes, when it heard us, its ears

hurt. The mathematician measured the parabola of his memory
trying to find an equal sign in the ebbing waves.

The security guard had crossed his arms over his chest and stood up.
The tide could come in, but only so far. Little flowerets

of his younger self cartwheeled behind him. There was no way
he'd let himself go under again. After allowing a drop

of her late husband's laughter to dissolve on her tongue,
the widow looked long at the ocean. *Bigger,* she said,

much bigger than that. The woman who baked the cake
was on her knees with the miner, icing his resolve to haul up

whatever was buried. The ocean complied by filling in
each hole he'd dug until he realized the treasure he was seeking

was kneeling right there beside him. Between the sunset
and their kiss, we didn't know where to look! The insomniac

didn't want to hear anything above the alarm clock of her heart.
The waves, she claimed, made her feel too rushed. And the carpenter,

the carpenter pushed us away when we realized he was crying.
Everything I've ever made, he said, *can float.*

TWENTY-NINE

We wondered what good was a democracy
if we couldn't vote winter away. We were becoming

argumentative and spent a whole afternoon
throwing snowballs at the sun. We had grown tired of its

sulk. And snow! You can imagine the time we wasted
before the shovel was invented. Yelling hot words

into it, holding candles up to its girth. Who in god's name,
we wanted to know, invented such long driveways?

Accountability was the new stranger in town
and everyone wanted to have a drink in its company.

At first, we thought winter was just another ploy
the ocean was using to spy on us. A disguise it wore

to get closer to our windows. Without any rain to drink,
women were getting testy and refused to stir anything in a pot,

which meant our children, who were still growing at an alarming rate,
were getting hungrier and refused to be liaisons between our demands

and the clouds. We were getting desperate and called the lifeguards
who stood before the sea of snow with their hands held out.

Neighbour, they said in a soothing tone, *give us back the grass
and trees you have swallowed.* If winter wasn't the ocean disguised,

it was closely related— it had the same eyes. Steely.
And it was tight-lipped, winning the staring contest we weren't sure

who started. We stepped back when it started melting,
like the predictions had warned, into something resembling water.

It's true, we squandered the ocean as a form of grandeur
in our talk. We'd spend several oceans, for example,

when boasting of our love. The promise of swimming
seven oceans to get a job done became a standard contractual

obligation when negotiating road or roof repair. But it was
our children who were responsible for taking it to the conversational

level insisting their joy was tidal and their anger came in waves.
They told time by the grain when they were unhappy

and by the beach when they were. And unlike our several oceans,
their love was one sweet river heading deeper and around the tender

corner of further away from home. We became the uncool parents
greeting them enthusiastically with marshland and clams

proving again how algaed we were, how barnacled.
Don't dance in front of us, they'd say,

*you wouldn't believe how shipwrecked you look
and how far out to sea, crab-legs.*

THIRTY-ONE

We had to drink spilled moon from the lake for courage
to face the ocean with our request. We had tried many times

to speak to it but the ocean was part landlord, part wolf
and rarely took us seriously. Its heavy hands sometimes felt

inclined to hold us under until bright lights squirted
from our hearts and mercy was a plea we'd have no choice

but to hitch to. Often it left us clues we tried solving,
our scientists and poets convening in a boardroom

with the washed up rubber boot, the purple chew toy
of its soliloquy. Those were the years the poets wrote epics

concerned with bedlam, dogs and heavy hearts. The only solace
we were getting was from our children, those little motors

for the knock-knock joke. This is when the ocean began appearing
in our dreams, often disguised as our mothers or hooded strangers

with something important to say, but when they opened their mouth
to speak, fish would swim out. The era of uncertainty had begun.

Our plan was to stand before the ocean with the small hook
of our intent, but when we did come face to face with it,

we found ourselves leaning in, having no choice
but to listen.

THIRTY-TWO

We had been feeding thin wafers
of moonlight to our daughters. No one

had warned us of the danger
or the potency of this new fad diet.

But show me a pine tree now and I'll show you
one of our girls. Those cones of persistence;

the sharp needles of argument. Stubborn and green,
green, green. Upward and outward. First they wanted

kittens. Now they want a clean ocean.
They wore their disdain like lip gloss

and flirted with the security cameras
of their fears. Their talk belied their curfews

and they insisted on wearing their grandmothers'
watches. Nothing could make them hurry.

Some of us studied them and now put on
our boots as if every morning is a mountain

not yet tamed. We'd kept our growls on a leash
for so long, when we let them loose they kept looking back

at us. Our girls taught us the right way
to spoon the spilled stars. The infusion

of outer space with the darker oil of our secrets
made us heady with abandon. We fell into the arms

of our daughters as if we'd been lost at sea
and they were the ones standing on shore

to welcome us: grass huts lit with composure.
They'd built a fire, burning everything we had ever

taught them. They had no choice, they explained,
it was the only way they could imagine keeping us warm.

THIRTY-THREE

Because the ocean's motor never wore out,
we knew we were in the presence of something

special. We brought it gifts of fancy earrings because,
so often, we treated it like an ear. We brought it

coins for the jukebox it sometimes was. Our poets
claimed the ocean was an edit of its former self,

that it once was bejewelled with a great many more
adjectives and went on like a dirge. Some of us

painted our lips and breasts with it. We wanted
to wear it like a badge or flag; we wanted to be

an edited version of our former selves, and like it,
we wanted to keep moving with clouds at our back

and an implication of orcas beneath our talk.

THIRTY-FOUR

It became the broth of our prayers but its waves broke
against our idea of home and we grew afraid.

There were conspiracy theorists who believed
it was invented to remind us that our own motors

were lacking and that the funeral industry was behind it.
The astronomers simply continued pointing to the sky

and the lifeguards coughed all the last breaths they'd caught
in their collective mouths and in this way birthed

the Milky Way, which didn't give us any answers
but finally gave us reason for reverie. When our daughters turned up

in our dresses, wanting to borrow some ocean
for their own lips and breasts, we had to sit down.

They were a surprise of shamelessness and shrug,
going out with a mind of their own, kissing

whoever they damn well pleased, undressing to show off
their newly acquired shoreline.

THIRTY-FIVE

It was our last-born sons and daughters who
untethered the boats while we slept and left

like birds on the ocean's back. Their notes explained
how tired they were of our fear. How it diminished

the flashlights of their laughter and plucked feathers
from their plump and bashful joy. The ocean

accessorized their party clothes with a dark hat
and they were determined to get to the bottom of it

which was exactly what we were afraid of.

We went to the woman whose son had long ago
set off in a stolen boat to never return. It was said

the stones around her garden birthed our worries.
The clouds over her house were suitcases packed

with our rain. She brewed a drop of his laughter
with a handful of mint. She unfolded a tablecloth

and set spoons beside the cups. There was a magnetic
field of slowness around her that was contagious.

Some of us stirred honey into our cups for what felt like
hours. At our first swallow, the small dose of his laughter

chased itself down a hill and rolled in the grass, braying
the green of springtime. The vapour of it fogged our eyes

with tears. We'd been too busy to harvest any of our own
children's laughter and had been drinking our mint empty.

We were impressed by how she'd ironed the sadness
out of her voice and steamed open her fears. The way

she'd preserved the choicest strawberry of moments
and scrubbed all the scolding from the corners.

We wanted to ask her how she managed but our voices
were small mice compared to our loneliness.

I dream sometimes that he swims beside me,
she told us, *and if I'm lucky, I can feel*

the nudge of him. You see, she said, *I made many mistakes.*
I thought I was his ocean and, foolishly, he, my fish.

THIRTY-SEVEN

According to our scholars, the newly birthed Milky Way
was rhinestoned with souls, which proved the soul's

existence. The lifeguards, when asked, said they'd tasted
the hard candy of the soul when they tried reviving

an ocean victim. But we'd always been suspicious of souls.
We knew they could escape because we often heard

their hooves, the slap of their tails. They'd wander off
at night and when we'd wake, we'd feel emptier,

our great finned souls swimming against the current
and further away. We'd cover our mouths when we laughed,

when we yawned. Once they broke out, souls were just a nuisance
to coax back. There was a trap of words the poets had sugared

and we'd take classes to learn how to enunciate without sounding
desperate. When they returned, we'd have to swallow our souls

like the pit of a plum or a vitamin. It could take several days
to feel enriched, to see the sky in the puddles again.

THIRTY-EIGHT

Souls became the perfect distraction. We had to keep
their gowns clean. We had to buff their moods.

But some of us were wounded in a way that made our days
need crutches. We were invalids in the pale hospital hours

of our kitchens. No one had warned us that our children
would leave and we were bereft, holding up the bedclothes

of their childhood and breathing deep the pink lambs
of their voice. We had no choice but to steal the poets' trap

of sugared words and meet at the ocean. Bravely, we tried
reciting them without sounding desperate. That our souls

were grazing on the hill behind us no longer mattered.
We wanted to lure our wandering children home.

The words we used had the thin syrup of our loneliness
in their veins. In this way, we learned that words also have souls,

and when the souls of our words escaped, there was a glitter
frosting the ocean, and briefly, we had managed to sugar its tide.

THIRTY-NINE

It was soon obvious we shouldn't have drunk
the lake water greased in moonlight. It woke

the bears hibernating in us and got us back on
our feet. We scavenged the silence looking

for the berries of our original names. We tore open
old arguments, rooting through accusations

hungry for meat. We barged into the idea of home
and ransacked its coziness. Things weren't going

as we had planned. What was this thing happening to us?
The way someone would just drop like a tree.

The way someone would clutch at their heart
as if the ferry leaving with all their true words

was sinking. The ocean ignored us. The moon.
The elders were puzzled and consulted the dry sand

with their tears. They counselled patience
but we had sipped the moon-steeped lake

and our anger refused to sleep in a cave.
It was grizzly and wanted to claw open our innards

until this ravaging hunger to know was soothed.

We crushed the menthol shade of pine trees
and drank it brewed to soothe them. We raked up

the underside silence of rocks and breathed
in the mystery to overwhelm them. We caught

them as soon as they left our mouths and threw them
on the fire. They'd burn to spark but still,

our questions wouldn't rest. They patrolled
the fenced edge of everything we knew

and shone their flashlights into the dark.
We'd gather at the ocean and tried tossing

them in, hoping they'd drown. In this way,
we were immortal. They could swim. They'd kick

up every unturned routine, wake up every sleeping
doubt. They made our hands pace and introduced

the idea of cliffs to our sleep. What was it they wanted
to know? We sometimes had to sit with them

when they grew infirm and far too weak to be of any
use. We always knew when one had wandered too far

and would no longer be able to return. At first, we'd celebrate,
but always a dark silence would follow.

The era of discord had begun, often described as the age of:
why did you call me a bitch? Because you called me a dickhead.

An age that could easily go on forever. There was a gas station
of strawberries to buy at the edge of summer but who wanted to

slow down once merged onto the highway of the possibility?
The horizon behind us was a persistent cloud of headlines

and all we had was the insurance of car seats and a national anthem.
Love, if it was organic, could still be sprayed over the low orchard

about to ripen into a U-pick of desire. Sure, we could find our way
to each other in the dark but the way was a tired groove

in the linoleum of our domestic bliss. We needed more monkeys
and mangos, our therapists insisted. We needed to absorb our dickheadedness

and be grateful for our bitchiness. Look at us: we took roads
and chairs for granted until they fell apart. And because the ocean

refused to be canned or shipped, homesickness became chronic,
viral even: we achooed, adieued all over each other.

We invented seances after we discovered death
but were amateurs at communication. Our voice memos

were essentially us saying what we didn't want to forget
into our empty beer steins and then drinking the vapour of it.

Hopeful. Seances were louder. We'd call a name into the night
and then wait for that person to respond. You could see

how this created rich opportunity for the invention of things
like the practical joke. Divorce. And anger management classes.

We held meetings to find out where people went when they died
because none of them were answering us. The poets presented

the metaphor of an empty boat drifting on the sea. The drama club
quickly turned the metaphor into a musical we enjoyed watching

but it left us no closer to knowing. Death terrified us. And surrounded
by clocks the way we were, we were constantly running out of time.

We elected a committee to ask the ocean what it knew. Reticent
sixteen-year-old girls agreed to join only after being promised

tongue piercings and hair extensions. They were our gold,
walking the way they did, inventing the new language of the written laugh-

out-loud, happy faces freckling everything they touched.
Eventually we realized we'd need a translator to talk to them.

They'd often speak in shrugs, their looks singeing any feathers
we had left on us. They intimidated everyone but the ocean.

It was aloof as they were, tasting everything with its tongue.

FORTY-THREE

For a long time we waited for our dead to return.
We tied scraps of one-sided conversations to trees

so they'd feel compelled to reply. We steeped tea
from their favourite hours and softened the wind

with the smells of baking. We set our tables
with the hearty stew of proposals, the flaky pastry

of apologies. We stuck our pipes with the tobacco
of their names and lit our voices to call them

with smoke. We missed them and often saw them
in dreams. They'd point to wolves and howl the first few chords

of winter or sit cradled in shade sending down tender leaves
for this fresh new salad of a summer without them.

We consulted the ocean but it was either a furrowed
brow or a pacing waiting room. Against our will,

we'd pick up from where we'd been left but always
further away and always without.

FORTY-FOUR

It was easy to tell when someone had forgotten
to thoroughly wash a name out before using it again.

The process was simple though time-consuming.
It involved a complete turn of tide, anchoring a piece of linen

with the name stitched on it and waiting for the ocean
to eat off the bones of its former memories: the tenderloin

of the person's voice, the sugar crust of their laugh,
the whipped cloud of their whisper. In this way, the ocean

served us. But it was difficult for some, knowing what they were
giving up. Giving up is so different than taken away

and we were poorly schooled for both. Some still boiled
the linen and drank the tea of their longing.

Some wore the linen stitched to the underside of their shirts,
so their hearts could take small breaths of its echo.

And some, when saying the name over a newborn's head,
were impatient for the child to grow so they could once again hear

the caramel of that laugh, run their fingers through the nougat
of their whispers; the clear sky of reunion exiled behind everything

they would do.

Things really changed when we learned to comb
the moonlight off the pasture of an evening ocean

and harvest it for the married couples. It was an age
of *au contraire*, of the meaningful stare, of everywhere.

Love had been left a fallow field after the crop of our children
ripened into opinionated adults craving a longer and brighter story

than their childhood chalk could provide. Oh, the coniferous tears
of our pining. The fish hooks of our goodbyes. We bought moving tape

by the decades and boxed up the bath times and the curfews,
planted the bunny plates in the orchards and then ate

the surprising fruit of this new silence. Our bodies perked their ears then
at the succulent hunger beneath the pelt of our hours. We had a caravan

of spare rooms and a gypsy of kisses. We peeled our old routines
until the sweetness at their core made our hands sticky. We stole

each other's hearts and threw caution to the wind. Our houses
may have been empty but our pantries were full.

We basted decadence, flambéed it and then dipped it
into excuses. We poured the lava from our secrets

into foil cups and presented them as declarations
to each other. We plugged into electrical storms

and marched our arguments down Main Street.
We sat at the edge of bottomless and fished out

the last living things. We knew better than anyone.
We had invented corkscrews, hadn't we? We'd invented

twist-off caps. When we poured the first vat of pavement
into our sense of adventure, some of us spit into it

for luck. Others turned their backs and in this way,
political parties were invented. Spending came next.

In order to properly see the sunset we had to order
special glasses. Moonlight was the original facial cream.

And now that we had roads, we could go anywhere.
Escape. We wrote notes to our young children, explaining

the best defrosting methods and invented psychology
to soothe the teddy bears of their bedtimes.

The maternal necessity of invention required the invention
of couches then, for the psychology to work. Everything

is connected! Toll booths came from the ancient concept
of slowing down. Tokens and speeding was our retort,

a kind of "fuck you" to the concept. You can already see
how feisty we were becoming.

FORTY-SEVEN

We didn't want to be here, we wanted to be
there. We had trampled here, tarnished the shine

of its puddles and overfed the small fauns
of its future. We loosened our pants

and took to the couch. Our malaise created
a thick fog and though we couldn't see the ocean,

we knew it was out there, we could hear it
breathing. We organized an expedition team

gathering those of us willing to eat the raisins
of winter clouds and walk the uneven ground of our fear.

We stuffed our pockets with the echoes
of family mealtimes that we'd eat like apples

when we were lonely. We brought map-making
equipment and magnifying glasses for our voices.

We seasoned our shadows with cinnamon
and neatened our names with a comb. We practised

our handshakes. We would walk until we got there.
Some said it was dissent that came disguised

as a question, others said it was the origin of the joke:
Where did you say you were going? There.

But where? Bedford then, was either founded
by exasperation or a serious need to sit down.

Tourism was great until the ocean went all coyote on us.
Lurking behind schoolyards, attacking people.

We were told to act big. To stand aggressively in our place.
Experts in animal control told us we had polluted its natural habitat

with our motored hands and greasy mayor. It had to feed further
afield and was too wild to mediate. The marriage counsellors

suggested we do five random kind things for it on a weekly basis
until it trusted us again. Also, to show we were listening,

we were to "mirror" what it was saying. We gave that job
to the poets. Apparently, it was "a tired bus driver"

and "a wayward friend." It was "the midnight of the death
of nights" and "the orphanage we'd been taken from."

A fourth grade class made it their Spring Fling project.
With glitter glue and feathers, we were given murals

of how our life should look. We'd need more diving boards,
exploding rainbows and smiling dolphins/unicorns to achieve

any of it. The mothers of teenage boys elected themselves
to counsel. They wore wedge shoes and pink nail polish

and were either fiercely tired or determined to get supper on,
nodding while we explained how it sprawled its stuff everywhere.

How it stayed up until all hours of the night and gave us no
respect. Sound familiar, we asked. They leaned in as if over a map:

you are here, they said, manicured but in the trenches, *trust us,
let go of any ideas of what you think it should be doing.*

The harbour didn't like being held captive by the shadows
of our buildings. We treated it well but still its dorsal fins

weakened and flopped. The tide was nothing more than
a sleepy scratch of water up over rocks

and then a yawn back down. The balls we threw to it
sank. It stopped slurping, it stopped nibbling.

It hardly growled. Some days it looked like a carpet,
other days, a flooded campsite: disks of paper plates,

lipsticked cigarette butts, the wet embers
of our vacations. What was the fun of these skyscrapers

if the only view we had was a petulant body of water?
We bought fish from the market to feed it. The older women

crocheted the most tender dialogue skimmed from our dreams,
carrying afghans by the armload down to its shore.

In this way, they invented nets and managed to catch
the grit of starlight from previous nights. With the right amount

of sugar and boiled darkness, we soon had vats
of a nectar so potent it bubbled. It wasn't that we got drunk

but forgetful and became so greedy for more, we over-fished
our dreams for their tenderness. When poverty arrived,

we were down to the bones of our talk. If we rubbed
two sticks together, briefly we'd be nourished by the smell

of their wood.

We'd been jilted, left at the harbour. Our wild lover;
our reckless friend. Our raison d'être had transformed

into a bland and mild version of itself. It was a lion
pacing beneath the bridges, the grid of condo shadows.

It was a mangier version of itself, its surface lacklustre
and its growl, without the saw teeth of threat, was senior.

It had been taught to go down on its knees, to climb
on the chair, leap through fire and recite the seasons.

It was like a dog dressed in finery. And you know the way ears
can give away so much of what an animal is thinking?

If it had ears, they'd have slid down its head by now,
quivering.

The gulls threaded their flight into the needle eye of expanse
and mended up its waves. The moon spread its cream

on the flood of its forehead, smoothing its worry lines
and nets. An invalid in the pale room of a summer

morning. Thirsty and thin. We wrung our hands.
It had been fevered, its complaints as unheeded as last season's upturned

boats. Waking us in the night, it had stood at the end of our beds,
bewildered and tousled. Baby, we had called it. Go back

to sleep. It was one of our last frontiers. A moving picture
of presence. Some couldn't look long at it without

an immigration of tears. Others felt the belligerent
burn of their predicament, trying to back out of a narrow

parking space and into the pilgrimage of their plans. It had been
a patient mirror while we fixed our hair, looked into our mouths.

The clouds traveled upon it without leaving a wake.

We woke one morning and the ocean was gone. Some of us
were relieved. Who can blame it if it had been our audience?

We kept forgetting our lines and driving into the props.
If we were the audience then its dramatic monologue was going on

forever. It was either all plot or all character. Setting,
if you were a landscape artist. You can see how difficult

a relationship it was. We'd never met anything so stoic.
Decisive yet meandering. The birds that would occasionally

break free of it were the same birds that dove back into it.
The get-me-out-of-here, wait-come-back of the original codependent

relationship. We accused the gamblers of losing it. We thought the priests
had prayed it away. That our sad choir had practised too close to it

and had sent it packing with their long, but harmonious, dirges. Our relief
soon turned to indignation. How dare it leave us with all of this

to care for. We imagined it vacationing at some resort
while we were stuck here with a restless moon that refused

to settle on anything.

FIFTY-THREE

We drummed on our dreams and smoked the sleep
of the predator birds. We took counsel from the dry

sand. We boiled fistfuls of grass and drank the green broth,
tasting the echo of its last rain. We measured teaspoons

of the stories behind our tears and wrung the dew
from the morning mist. We steeped apologies

for the sap of forgiveness at their core. We roasted
old arguments until they were completely dried out

and then wore them as shoes. Children were given crayons
and instructed to make welcome banners. Boats panted

on their ropes. Spoons were silent propellers geared up
to start a current. We had become the new tide: leaning in

to call the ocean then leaning back to watch it come.

Without the ocean, the animals of our dreams
prowled our sleep, denting our rest with their hooves

and horns. They howled, clawing at the doors of our dark hours.
We'd wake to discover their baying had lowered the clouds

and accused winter of shoplifting the last of the summer light
they so loved to drink. We had collected bones from the shore

but the creature they formed defied our understanding.
Had we got everything wrong? When we looked at pictures

we'd taken with the ocean behind us, we were startled by how unhappy
it appeared, how stricken. We were left with a heavy feeling

that we had, somehow, let it down. When it wanted to sing,
we had insisted it keep doing its work. Our hunger had many mouths

and there were fish to clean.

FIFTY-FIVE

Our elders insisted the ocean was still there.
That we were born with a seed of it and when we spoke,

its waves pressed against our words for a further shore.
But we had let ourselves become sub-divided and suburban,

buckling our talk into seat belts, mad always for safety.
When had our schedules become the new mountains?

We were doing our best to ignore how grey our memories
were becoming, how stooped and hard of hearing our laughter was.

The ocean, apparently, was right in front of us and we were dropping
like flies. We bought the dried flower tops of our politicians'

explanations. We tuned our radios to the sunsets and downloaded
whale call overdubbed with protest songs. Our intent was good,

but with air bags. The poets rigged antennas to the antique words
of gratitude with a jalapeño of the unexpected but we were tired

of the poets. They were chesterfields or they were curtains.
We wanted pure ocean podcast into our veins but tethered

while we slept. We wanted death to be a stranger we'd never have to
give directions to. We consulted the beekeepers infamous

for not getting stung but they were in a meeting with the poets.
We consulted the gamblers but they wanted to see us only to raise us

ten. Our voices were rarely coming home covered in mud anymore.

Filmmakers had started making films of the ocean
in 3D. Scratch and sniff coastal cards were sold

at lottery booths. Material for dresses was cut with the froth
of tide in mind. We had wanted the ocean to be the new

flavour, the new sound. We'd drive for miles to get a glimpse
of it because, let's face it, it revitalized the part of us

we kept rooting for, that apple seed of energy that defied
multiple choice career options. The ocean had egged the best part

of us on. And it scared us. We never knew what it was thinking
and spent thousands on specialists who could make predictions.

And the predictions always required hard hats and building permits,
furrowed eyebrows and downward trends. Why is it so hard

to trust something that leaps, disappears and then reappears
spouting more light? When had our hearts become badly behaved

dogs we had to keep the screen door closed to? Have you ever run
along its shore, the pant of it coming closer? And that feeling

that yipped inside of you, the Ginger Rogers of your feet, your ability
to not get caught then, yes, get soaked. Didn't you feel like it was

part of your pack? When it whistled, whatever it is in you
that defies being named, didn't that part of you perk up?

And didn't you let it tousle you to the ground,
let it clean between your ears before it left you?

Wasn't that all right? That it left you? That we all will?

ACKNOWLEDGEMENTS

Ocean is dedicated to: Stephens Gerard Malone, Stephanie Domet, Carsten Knox, Tara Thorne and especially to Penelope Jackson who got a babysitter, so insisted we read. ¶ I'd like to thank Pete, Leisha, Colin, Ryan and Robyn (love, love). ¶ My friend Helen Humphreys. ¶ My teachers, all of them. ¶ My students, all of them. ¶ My co-workers in the creative program at Dalhousie University and at WFNS. ¶ Gaspereau Press. ¶ Connotation Press and The Malahat Review: Essential East Coast Writing for publishing a version of some of these poems. ¶ The Canada Council for the Arts and Arts Nova Scotia. ¶ Italo Calvino, Charles Olson, Neko Case, Bookmark Bookstore, Lynn Emmanuel, The Laughing Whale Coffee Roasters, Louise Bogan, Propellor Brewery, Lorca, Local Source, FRED, The Young Thrillionaires, Jaime Forsythe, The Company House, René Char, Phil Hall, Barry Dempster, Ben Gallagher, Dee Dee's Ice Cream, Shandi Mitchell, The Dartmouth Ferry, Tig Notaro, The MacDonald Bridge, its twin: the McKay, The Halifax Harbour, The Banff Centre, Good Food Emporium, Nuri Bilge Ceylon, Werner Herzog, Pina Bausch, Marina Abramović, The Food Wolf, Cy Twombly, Alan MacLeod, Dharma Sushi, Bill Wood, Roy Ellis, Compagnie Marie Chouinard, NSCAD, Morris East, Etta James, Lawrencetown Beach, Video Difference, Sue Gillis, Warren Heiti, Darren Bifford, Hutten Family Farm, Krista Peters, The Seaport Farmers' Market, Emma Brown, Chris Penney, Crowbar Real Foods, Jack Julian, Sam Hickox, Ryan Murphy, Steve-o-Renos, Dave Dahms, Daniel Rainham, Mik Owens, Rose Cousins, The Salt Marsh Trail, Jan Morrison, Sophie Pilipczuk, Susanne Brown, Ace Burgers, Lori, Brian, Henri and Charlie DeBlois, Dots and Loops, Pam Goyette, Jordan and Meghan Underwood, The Brewery Market, Carolyn Whelan, Dru Donavan, The North End, Catlin Smith, CBC, Ryan Turner, Kathleen Martin, Andrew Steeves, Gary Dunfield, Trina Adam. And you.

AN INDEX OF OPENING LINES

Some politicians wanted a wider shore so more people could visit our city ... TWENTY-TWO

Souls became the perfect distraction ... THIRTY-EIGHT

The barbers taught us how to trim the trees ... TWENTY-SIX

The era of discord had begun, often described as the age of: why did you call me a bitch? ... FORTY-ONE

The gulls threaded their flight into the needle eye of expanse and mended up its waves ... FIFTY-ONE

The harbour didn't like being held captive by the shadows of our buildings ... FORTY-NINE

The idea of courting began after a group of us smoked the exhaust from a pride of children imagining they were lions ... THIRTEEN

The idea of home was so big, so bottomless, carpenters had to tie a rope around their waists ... NINE

The incline to our streets was first invented as an easy way to feed the ocean ... FIVE

The more it ate of us, the less we liked it ... TWENTY-THREE

The ocean is the original mood ring ... SEVENTEEN

The original lifeguards were taught to address the ocean as neighbour ... TWENTY-FOUR

The real estate agent chewed gum to cover the smell of bank on his breath ... ONE

There were many stories about what was going on beneath its surface ... SIXTEEN

The trick to building houses was making sure they didn't taste good ... EIGHT

The weather has always been both a concern and conversation kindling ... NINETEEN

Things really changed when we learned to comb the moonlight off the pasture of an evening ocean and harvest it for the married couples ... FORTY-FIVE

Tourism was great until the ocean went all coyote on us. ... FORTY-EIGHT

We basted decadence, flambéed it and then dipped it into excuses ... FORTY-SIX

We crushed the menthol shade of pine trees and drank it brewed to soothe them ... FORTY

We didn't want to be here, we wanted to be there ... FORTY-SEVEN

We drummed on our dreams and smoked the sleep of the predator birds ... FIFTY-THREE

We first invented running so we could be in two places ... FOUR

This book was set in W. Ross Mills' Huronia type (with Jim Rimmer's
Dokument for display) by Andrew Steeves and printed offset and
bound under the direction of Gary Dunfield at Gaspereau Press.

7   6   5

Library and Archives Canada Cataloguing in Publication

Goyette, Sue
    Ocean / Sue Goyette.

ISBN 978-1-55447-122-5
    I. Title.

PS8563.O934O34 2013   C811'.54   C2013-900309-6

GASPEREAU PRESS LIMITED *e* GARY DUNFIELD
& ANDREW STEEVES *e* PRINTERS & PUBLISHERS
47 CHURCH AVENUE KENTVILLE NS B4N 2M7
Literary Outfitters & Cultural Wilderness Guides